DATE DUE

Demco, Inc. 38-293

THE ART OF
COLOR MIXING

A GRUMBACHER LIBRARY BOOK

INTRODUCTION

No other subject is as broad, as exciting, as satisfying to the painter as the study of color. It is a part of human existence in everything we see, in the clothes we wear, in the products we buy, in our enjoyment of what we consider beautiful and in our reactions and associations. Even the fledgling painter brings to his study of color a rich background of personal experience.

From the artist's viewpoint, the study of color can be greatly simplified if the boundaries of particular interest and application are defined in advance. The physicist studies color in light; the psychologist its emotional reaction as it relates to our sensory apparatus, and the chemist the physical properties of pigments. All of these areas could be of interest to the painter, but his primary concern, however, is color in its application to color relationships and color mixing. His immediate goal is the translation of his subjective and objective ideas into mixtures of pigments on a palette and their application to a canvas. He must begin, therefore, with the pertinent basic principles that will increase his skills.

In this book, the student is introduced to color principles and color mixing by experienced teachers whose demonstrations and explanations can lead the way to individual development and greater understanding of color.

MATERIALS

Although color mixing is employed in painting in the various media, it is discussed in this book in terms of oil colors because of their facility for demonstration and instruction. Oil paints lend themselves to the study of color theory and color mixing because they do not change appreciably in color from the wet to the dry state and, also, because mixtures can be adjusted without concern that the paints will become dry on the palette before a desired result is achieved. Brushes are many and varied. The bulk of painting in oil is done with bristle brushes, and it is best for the beginner to stay with these. Sables (soft hair brushes) are excellent but when not properly used, or overused, will tend to make the work slick or fussy.

To supplement the text and provide quicker reference we include here a brief glossary.

ACHROMATIC: Black, white and grays. Work executed without color.

CHROMA: The relative hue intensity of a color.

GLAZE: Color thinned to a transparent state and applied over previously painted areas to modify the original color. (See also Underpainting)

GOUACHE: (Tempera) Opaque watercolors and the technique of painting with such colors using white to make tints.

HIGHLIGHT: Those small areas on a painting or drawing on which reflected light is the brightest.

HUE: That attribute which describes colors by name, i.e. red, blue, etc.

IMPASTO: A manner of painting in which the paint is laid on thickly so that texture stands out in relief.

MEDIUM: The material used for a drawing or painting, i.e. Oils, Water Colors, Pastels, etc. Any substance added to color to facilitate application or to achieve a desired effect.

SHADE: Color made darker by the addition of black.

TINT: Color made lighter by the addition of white. The result of applying a wash or glaze over a white surface.

UNDERPAINTING: Preliminary painting used as a base for textures or for subsequent painting or glazing.

VALUE: Relative lightness and darkness.

WASH: A highly fluid application of color.

Designed and edited by Walter Brooks
Copyright ©1966 by M. Grumbacher, Inc.
460 West 34 Street, New York, N.Y.
Library of Congress Catalog Card Number 66-18998
Produced by Artists and Writers Press, Inc.
Printed in U.S.A. by Western Printing and Lithographing Co.

Turpentine, or an improved paint thinner, Grumtine, should be used to clean brushes, the palette, or mixed with linseed oil as a painting medium. Do not use the thinner excessively as a medium by itself since it tends to dilute the binder resulting in colors which may dust off when dry. A popular medium for oil painting is a mixture of turpentine and linseed oil.

The artists represented in this book, in the discussion of their palettes include colors not on the basic list which follows. You might want to add some of these other colors after you have gained confidence with this recommended list.

COLORS: Zinc Yellow (Lemon Yellow)   Yellow Ochre
       Cadmium Yellow, Medium   Burnt Sienna
       Cadmium Red, Light   Burnt Umber
       Alizarin Crimson   Thalo Green
       French Ultramarine Blue   Superba White
       Thalo® Blue

BRUSHES: (The brush style is designated by a letter following the series number.) This list will meet basic needs.
     F — Flats (flat, square-edge, long bristle) #2, #6, #10
     B — Brights (flat, square-edge, short bristle) #4, #8
     R — Rounds (round, pointed bristle) #6, sable #4
     L — Longs (flat, square-edge, long sable) #10
     Filberts — (flat, oval edge, long bristle) #4, #8

CANVAS: Fabrics prepared for painting. Available as panel, stretched on frames, or by the yard.

PAINTING KNIFE: A trowel-type flexible knife in a variety of shapes and sizes.

PALETTE: Wood, plastic, or disposable paper. A color mixing area. Also a personal selection of colors.

PALETTE KNIFE: For scraping palette clean and mixing colors. Can be used as a painting knife.

OIL CUP: Containers which can be clipped to the palette — one cup for the medium, the other for brush cleaner.

TURPENTINE (or Grumtine): For cleaning equipment and thinning mediums.

LINSEED OIL: The traditional "binder" for oil colors. Also used as a medium.

CHARCOAL: Either pencils or sticks. For preliminary sketching on canvas.

FIXATIVE SPRAY: For fixing charcoal drawing on canvas before painting. Available in spray cans (Tuffilm Spray) or for use with mouth atomizer.

PAINT BOX: A desirable piece of equipment for storing brushes, paint, palette, and accessories when painting outdoors.

EASEL: A support for the canvas during painting. Available as collapsible tripod, studio types and as combination sketch box units. In some sketch boxes the lids serve as easels.

R

F

B

B

F

Filbert

B

L

[3]

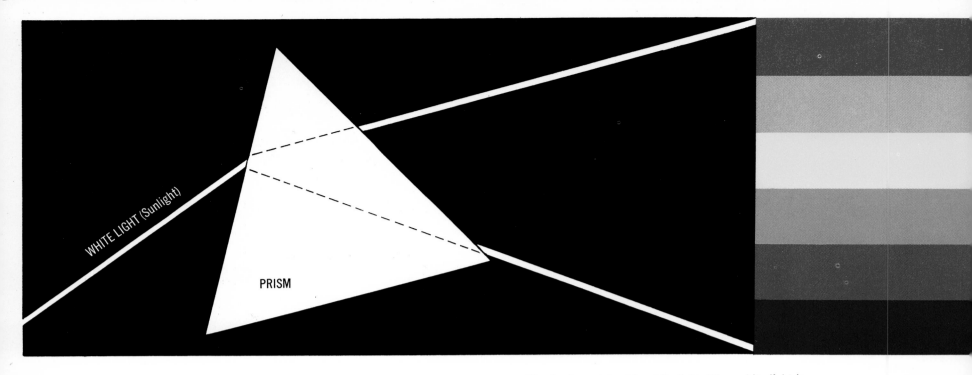

All color is contained in white light. When white light is passed through a crystal prism, it is dispersed into the spectrum range of visible colors. It also can be reestablished as white light.

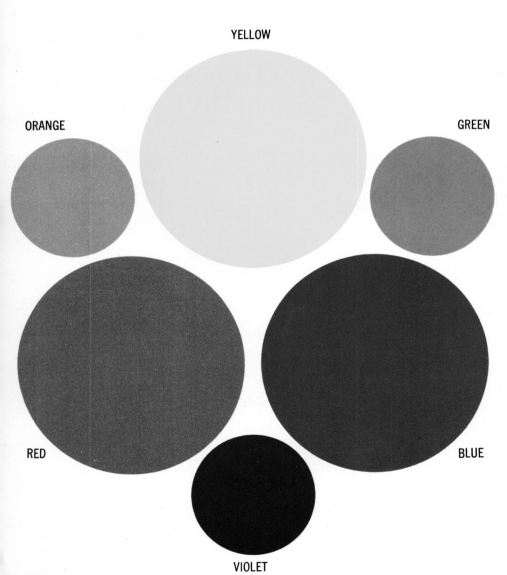

YELLOW

ORANGE

GREEN

RED

BLUE

VIOLET

In paint mixing, the entire range of the spectrum can be produced by the selective use of three primary colors: Red, Yellow and Blue. Unlike the **light spectrum,** which results in white light when all of its components are mixed, the **pigment spectrum** produces a dark value approximating black.

BASIC COLOR PRINCIPLES

All Color Theory is based on the principle that *color is light*. Normally, all of the colors we see are contained in the light reflected by pigments which, as chemical compounds, have the property of selectivity absorbing certain colors of the light spectrum. Thus, an object producing the visual sensation of *red* contains pigmentation which absorbs all of the colored rays of white light except the *red* which it reflects. *White* pigment absorbs none of the colored rays . . . while *black* absorbs all of the colors of the spectrum.

The nature of the illumination with which we work affects the colors we see. Natural light is not constant and the color bands of the spectrum are affected by the position of the sun due to the seasons of the year, the time of day and atmospheric conditions. Artificial light affects the appearance of colors because the spectrum range of each type of artificial light is determined by the physical nature of the light source (fluorescent, incandescent, etc.).

As an illustration of this phenomenon, examine simultaneously two paint-outs of an identical color: one under fluorescent, and the other under incandescent light. Notice the obvious difference.

This very elementary knowledge of what color is accepted to be is all that we, as painters, need to know about the physics of color.

(continued on page 6)

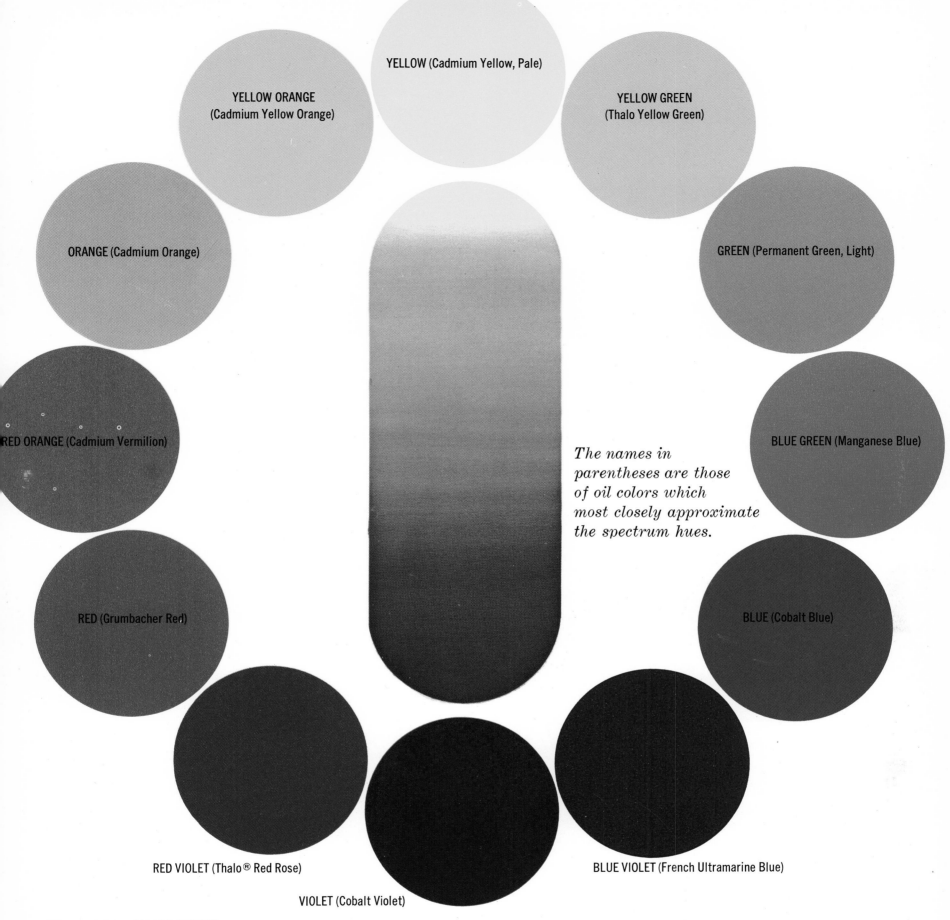

YELLOW (Cadmium Yellow, Pale)

YELLOW ORANGE (Cadmium Yellow Orange)

YELLOW GREEN (Thalo Yellow Green)

ORANGE (Cadmium Orange)

GREEN (Permanent Green, Light)

RED ORANGE (Cadmium Vermilion)

The names in parentheses are those of oil colors which most closely approximate the spectrum hues.

BLUE GREEN (Manganese Blue)

RED (Grumbacher Red)

BLUE (Cobalt Blue)

RED VIOLET (Thalo® Red Rose)

BLUE VIOLET (French Ultramarine Blue)

VIOLET (Cobalt Violet)

THREE PRIMARY COLORS SYSTEM

The simplest and most widely accepted method of applying color theory to painting is by means of the **Three Primary Colors System.**

A Color Wheel is an effective way of demonstrating this system. All the principal and intermediate hues of the light spectrum are represented on the Wheel by a series of 11 equidistant segments formed into a continuous band of 12 by the addition of Red Violet, which is missing from the light spectrum.

PRIMARY COLORS The three Primary Colors are: Red, Yellow and Blue.
SECONDARY COLORS The three Secondary Colors are: Orange, Violet, Green. Each is midway between the Primaries from which it can be mixed.
INTERMEDIATE COLORS The remaining colors are intermediates obtained by mixing adjoining Primary and Secondary Colors.
TERTIARY COLORS These represent a mixture of Secondary Colors.

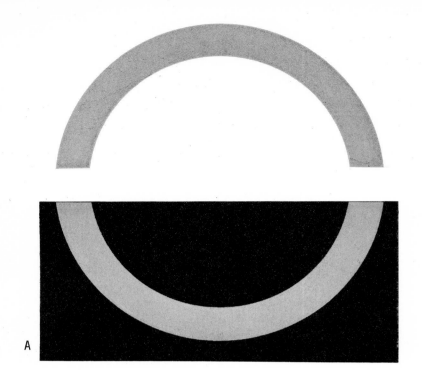

A

The effect of background on an **achromatic value** can be seen in A. This effect is also true with color values. In contrast with black, the curved line of gray gives the impression of being lighter than against white.

Although each value in B is all of one tone, the illusion of gradation of value at the edges is the result of contrast with the adjacent values.

The heightening of contrast in C gives the effect of the center circle being whiter than the surrounding white of the paper.

B

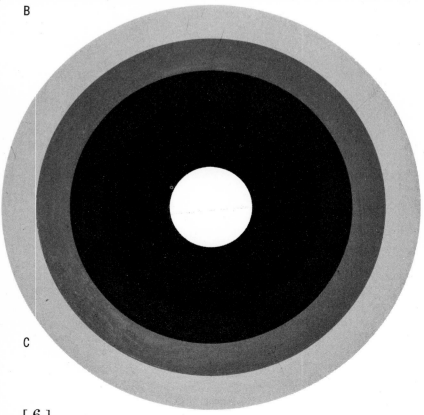

C

THE THREE DIMENSIONS OF COLOR

If we were to ask someone who has had little or no instruction in color theory to describe the difference between three colors: an intense Red, a dull Red, and a Yellow . . . his first reaction would undoubtedly be . . . "One color is Yellow and the other two are Reds." He might then further indicate that one of the two Reds is duller than the other. Finally, he might conclude that the Yellow is lighter than the Reds.

This layman's analysis describes, in the simplest terms, the three distinctly different and measurable characteristics of all colors, which are commonly known as the *Three Dimensions of Color.*

HUE . . . This is the most characteristic dimension which identifies a color by name, i.e., Red, Yellow, Blue, Blue Green, etc. Every color falls into a definite Hue category when related to the spectrum range of colors.

INTENSITY (also called *CHROMA*) . . . This dimension represents the relative intensity of hue. Colors of greater hue saturation can be described as being of higher Intensity than duller colors of the same hue dimension. For example, Burnt Sienna which the layman might describe as a Brown, is actually a relatively low intensity reddish Orange hue.

VALUE . . . This dimension represents the brightness of illumination and, under normal lighting conditions, locates a color's position in relation to a scale of grays between White and Black. A color such as an intense Yellow is light or high in value. An intense Violet is dark or low in value.

EACH OF THE THREE DIMENSIONS OF COLOR HAS A DEFINITE APPLICATION IN PAINTING.

Hue is important to the artist because of its psychological impact on the viewer. Moods of a picture may be emphasized by the selection of an appropriate range of hues. Yellows and Orange, associated with sunshine and warmth, are considered cheerful colors. Red, associated with fire, blood, etc., is usually thought of as a violent and exciting color. Blue, a cool color, connotates serenity, while Green implies restfulness and Violet is mysterious.

Normally, hues such as Red and Yellow are regarded as being *warm* and hues such as Blue and Blue Green are *cool.* This is a general color temperature classification, Although Thalo Red Rose is a warm color, it is cool when compared to Cadmium Vermilion.

Warm colors appear warmer and the cools seem cooler when contrasted with their opposites in temperature.

Warm colors tend to advance while cool colors seem to recede on the painted surface.

Intensity . . . This dimension is important because within a hue the artist can simulate depth and emphasize contrasts through variations in intensity.

In nature, under uniform lighting conditions, a color in the foreground will always appear more intense than the same color in the distance. The painter can also force colors to recede by reducing their intensity. A color will appear *more* intense when placed on or near a duller color of the same hue.

Value is the only dimension of color which can exist outside of color and is so represented by the scale of achromatic grays on page 8. Value is probably the most important dimension for the artist seeking to simulate form and effect emphasis through contrasts in light and shade.

The value of any color can be made lighter (*Tints*) by the addition of White or by means of a lighter color of the same hue. Colors which are made darker in value by the addition of a darker color of the same hue or by mixture with Black are called *Shades*. Both tints and shades, which represent distinct changes in the value dimension of a color, also tend to reduce the intensity and, in many instances, also effect its hue.

The painter should determine his lightest and darkest values and paint within this range. Light colors appear lighter against dark backgrounds and vice versa.

COLOR MIXING

Color mixing can *only* be learned through practical application and experimentation but a knowledge of color theory will give the beginner a basis for such application and experimentation.

To illustrate a problem in color mixing and its solution, let us assume that we are limited to a palette of three colors: Cadmium Yellow, Pale; Grumbacher Red and Cobalt Blue, plus Ivory Black and Zinc White. From this Primary selection, we are required to mix an Olive Green. As every color can be analyzed as to its relative Hue, Intensity and Value, Olive Green might be described as basically a *Yellow Green hue* of moderately *low intensity* and of approximately *middle value*. Our first step, therefore, in mixing this color is to blend the Blue and Yellow to produce a basic Yellow Green. This mixture results in a color of relatively high intensity. To reduce this intensity (*neutralize* this color), we have two choices:

A. We can add Red, the complement of Green, until the desired reduction of intensity is achieved (adjusting it with additional Blue, if necessary, because the true complement of Yellow Green is Red Violet). The resultant mixture may be too dark because as the intensity of a color is diminished by complementary mixture, its value is also lowered. Therefore, White may be required to adjust this dimension.

B. The alternate solution to this problem is to utilize a Gray, mixed from the Black and White, to reduce the intensity of the basic Yellow Green. Gray, employed to lower the intensity of any color, will not darken that color (unlike complementary mixtures), if it has the same value as the color. (continued on page 10)

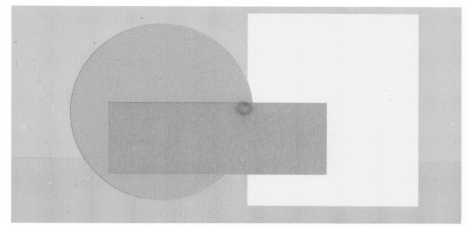

A

B

C

In the simple studies above can be seen some effects of value, intensity, and hue in painting. "A" is a high key arrangement with a close value range. The intensity is quite high in this analagous color scheme.

"B" is a low key arrangement (values in the lower end of the scale. The only intense color is the cold blue in this split-complementary scheme. "C" employs a wider value range, as well as greater variations in color temperature and color intensities. Notice how the warmer and more intense color areas appear to come to the fore.

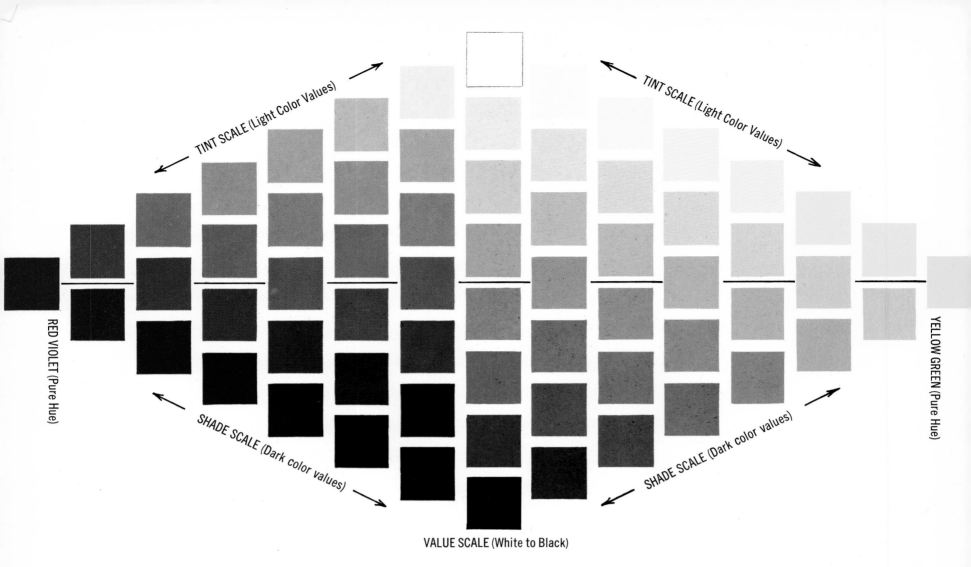

RED VIOLET (Pure Hue)

YELLOW GREEN (Pure Hue)

TINT SCALE (Light Color Values)

TINT SCALE (Light Color Values)

SHADE SCALE (Dark color values)

SHADE SCALE (Dark color values)

VALUE SCALE (White to Black)

The complements (Red Violet and Yellow Green) are at the ends of this diagram. The central line represents a **direct progression of complementary mixtures**. This is also demonstrated in the color wheel on page 5, showing the result of a mixture of the complements Yellow and Violet. Balanced color complements neutralize each other and produce gray or values approaching black. The achro-

matic **value scale** from white to black is in the center of the diagram. The **tint scale** (the upper diagonals of color) is white mixed with the pure color. The **shade scale** (lower diagonals) has black added to the pure color. The **intermediate steps** are the result of complementary mixtures tinted with white and shaded with black.

FULL STRENGTH COLORS

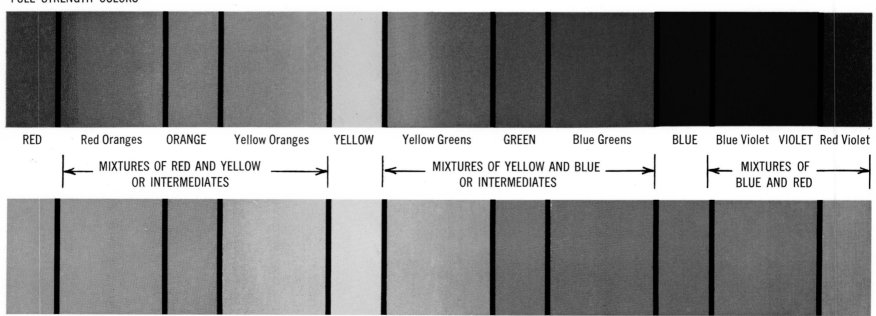

RED   Red Oranges   ORANGE   Yellow Oranges   YELLOW   Yellow Greens   GREEN   Blue Greens   BLUE   Blue Violet   VIOLET   Red Violet

◄——— MIXTURES OF RED AND YELLOW OR INTERMEDIATES ———►   ◄——— MIXTURES OF YELLOW AND BLUE OR INTERMEDIATES ———►   ◄——— MIXTURES OF BLUE AND RED ———►

TINTS (HIGHER VALUES) White added to full strength colors.

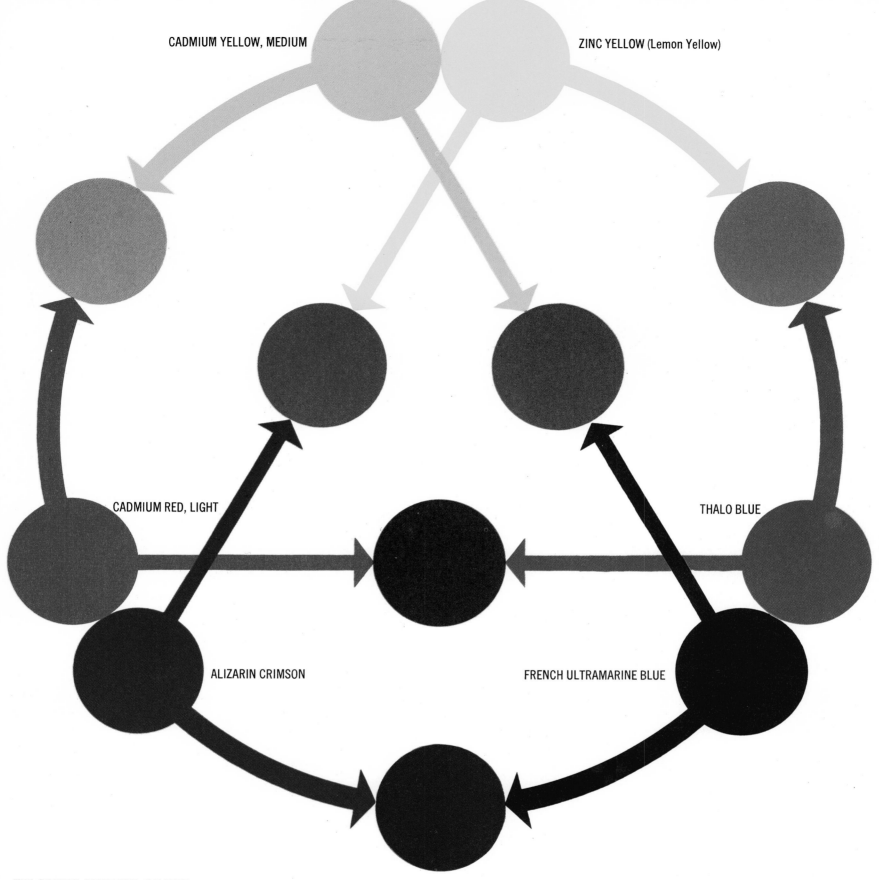

CADMIUM YELLOW, MEDIUM

ZINC YELLOW (Lemon Yellow)

CADMIUM RED, LIGHT

THALO BLUE

ALIZARIN CRIMSON

FRENCH ULTRAMARINE BLUE

THE DOUBLE PRIMARIES PALETTE

By selecting **two colors** for each of the three primary hue divisions of the spectrum, the degree of intensity of secondary mixtures can be controlled with much greater accuracy. For example, Thalo Blue and Lemon Yellow produce a variety of relatively intense greens. A second primary blue, French Ultramarine Blue, when mixed with Lemon Yellow produces progressively less intense greens, and this same French Ultramarine Blue when mixed with the second primary yellow, Cadmium Yellow, Medium produces a variety of greens which are still further reduced in intensity. This selective cross-combination of mixtures works just as effectively in all areas of the double-primaries palette. These colors are listed in the basic palette on page 3.

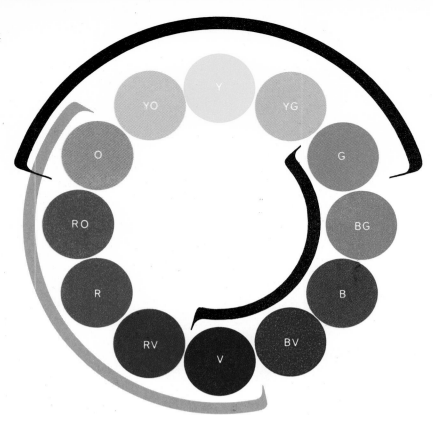

This diagram depicts an arbitrary selection of analogous colors, each group consisting of five colors balanced on a Primary. Analogous groupings can be selected from any segment of the circle and can be limited to as few as two colors.

The arrows in the diagram below indicate direct complements.
The shaded triangle indicates a split-complementary group.
The open triangle indicates a triadic harmony group.
The pointer can be rotated to any position on the circle and will locate similar color relationships.

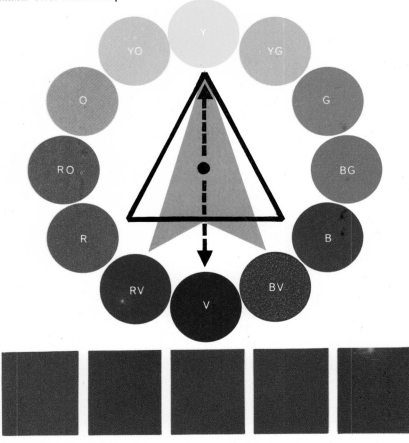

In this chart, Cobalt Blue has been reduced in intensity while value is maintained by the addition of Black and White. High intensity colors appear to advance and low intensity colors to recede.

(continued from page 7)

Artists' colors are produced in an extensive range of hues and intensities. The painter can readily select a palette of colors appropriate for any subject and thus, radically reduce the time and effort involved in color mixing.

The palette diagrammed on page 9 is an excellent selection for experimentation in color mixing. Study this carefully and test the various mixtures illustrated. Make your own tests with other combinations. Compare the tints produced by transparent applications on a white background and those, of equal value, made with the addition of White. Note the variations in the physical properties of each color, such as its tinting strength and degree of opacity or transparency.

It is impossible to judge accurately a color in isolation. A mixture which appears correct on the palette may not be so in relation to other colors when it is applied.

COLOR HARMONY

The mind normally attempts to equalize or neutralize the effect of extremes in stimuli because exposure to such extremes is disturbing. It is for this reason that the exercise of moderation is considered the keynote to harmony for all sensory perception.

Moderation can, however, become monotonous if the spice of variety is lacking. Accents of relatively acute extremes introduced into moderate diets of color, food, sound, odor or texture arouse and maintain interest.

There are three methods which may be used, *either separately or in combination*, to produce Color Harmony:

MONOCHROMATIC Harmony arrived at by utilizing one color plus White and Black. Certain subjects lend themselves to this color scheme. It is a challenging exercise that relies for effect upon the value and intensity ranges of a single hue within a painting.

COMPLEMENTARY Direct, *Split-Complementary* and *Triadic harmonies* represent relationships in color through the participation of all of the three Primaries in comparatively uniform visual distribution *(see diagram)*. However, it is suggested that in no combination should *all* of the colors be represented as fully intense. This is in accordance with the principle of moderation, because the three fully intense Primary Colors present in any such combinations actually represent the *extreme* condensation of the complete spectrum range. Thus, an intense Red Orange flower arrangement can be extremely effective against a pale Blue Green background which is relatively low in intensity. Should the Blue Green be too strong in hue, there would be a struggle for dominance with the Red Orange. The result might be somewhat discordant and disturbing.

When using complementary color schemes, handle them with restraint until you become more familiar with color.

ANALOGOUS (see diagram on page 10) These color harmonies are somewhat muted since only two of the three Primary colors are present in some combinations. In those instances where all three are present, two of them are in relatively weak concentrations. For example, at the Yellow segment of the color wheel, we might select an analogous grouping of Orange (*Yellow* + Red); Yellow Orange (*Yellow* + Red); Yellow; Yellow Green (*Yellow* + Blue) and Green (*Yellow* + Blue). By making one hue dominant in the painting . . . *Yellow* in this instance . . . and using adjacent colors with it, a pleasing balance can be maintained.

As an exercise in discovering the potentials of all of these color schemes, start by making abstract thumbnails.

Without undue concern for drawing or form, use monochromatic, complementary and analogous harmonies alone or in combination. This can give you a feeling for the value and color range necessary for harmonious effects. You will discover that the relationship between color areas of high or low intensity, as well as the value range within the painting are the keys to the success of any scheme.

The demonstrations through page 21 were prepared by Victor Kalin, noted painter and illustrator, who discusses technique as well as color in connection with still life and flowers.

In this painting are combined a number of popular, yet difficult objects for the student. Metals and glass offer the problems of texture with their sparkling well-defined highlights and elusive reflected colors. Apples, always a favorite subject, offer a challenge in the proper indication of subtle color and highlights within the form.

As shown in Step 1, the composition was sketched on the canvas with a little Yellow Ochre, thinned with turpentine. In Step 2, elements of the painting were then blocked in covering the canvas with areas of color as quickly as possible. The main reason for this is that a color may look correct against the background of white canvas, and can be completely out of key when neighboring colors are painted in. This process of color balancing is much easier in the early stages while the elements are merely blocked-in shapes and it is relatively easy to scrape off a color and replace it with another. (continued on page 12)

YELLOW OCHRE
ALIZARIN CRIMSON

FRENCH ULTRAMARINE BLUE
THALO GREEN
BURNT UMBER

CADMIUM RED, LIGHT
YELLOW OCHRE
THALO GREEN
WITH WHITE

The background was kept simple with subtle color changes within it for interest. Values were kept fairly light with no strong colors so that this area could act as a foil for the stronger, more chromatic colors and deeper play of value in the objects.

The drapery and copper container were painted as though there was nothing in front of them. The pitcher, because it is transparent, consists of little more than a few highlights and shadows to suggest its form. It is this subtle relationship between crisp highlights and darks that gives a painting of glass the qualities that suggest the brittle, shiny hardness of the material.

For the brass candlestick which presents the problem of painting a shiny metallic surface, Lemon Yellow and Burnt Umber were used in varying mixtures with Burnt Sienna for the warm color reflections on the side next to the large bronze bowl. The effect of brilliance in the candlestick is achieved by limited touches of very intense Lemon Yellow at the edge of the highlights.

It is interesting to note that although apples are usually thought of as being bright red, very little intense red is applied and in reality nearly all the colors found in the fruit are the result of mixtures of Yellow Ochre with Alizarin Crimson; Cadmium Red, Light; Yellow Ochre and Thalo Green.

When mixing colors to obtain a light tint, start with a quantity of white and add colors to it until you have the value you want. With darker or more intense colors, start with the color that is to be most dominant in the mixture and add color to this until you reach the mixture you want. Certain colors, you will find, are very powerful — a little goes a long way. Thalo Blue and Thalo Green are in this category. Test all of your colors by mixing small quantities with white and with each other to get a feeling for amounts needed in any mixture.

The mixtures above show combinations used to obtain some of the colors in the painting. For lighter, less intense tints, white was added to these colors.

YELLOW OCHRE
FRENCH ULTRAMARINE BLUE
BURNT UMBER
WITH WHITE

LEMON YELLOW
BURNT UMBER

THALO GREEN
YELLOW OCHRE
BURNT SIENNA
BURNT UMBER

BURNT SIENNA
FRENCH ULTRAMARINE BLUE

THALO GREEN
BURNT UMBER
WITH A TOUCH
OF WHITE

1

In painting a white object, the subtle play of value and color can be influenced by any number of conditions including: form, texture (dull or glossy—rough or smooth), color from the light source, and color reflected from surrounding objects. If you examine closely the colors reflected in a white china cup, you will discover that it catches light from several different sources, such as a window, an uncovered incandescent bulb or possibly a tinted lamp shade. It must, in reality, be lower in value than white in order to have the light areas appear sufficiently light. Even the highlights are not pure white, for they also contain some coloration from the light sources; the blue of the sky, or the warm tones of the electric light.

On the left can be seen the stages of laying in color for the painting on page 15 This subject deals with the problem of painting a white object.

In Step 1, the composition is sketched on the canvas using Yellow Ochre thinned with turpentine. In Step 2, color is blocked in on all areas of the canvas so that colors can be adjusted and balanced to each other as the painting develops.

2

In Step 3, the areas of the canvas have been blocked in and detail started in portions of the painting.

The pitcher was painted with an over-all color using French Ultramarine Blue, Burnt Sienna, and White. The jar, slightly warmer, was French Ultramarine Blue, Yellow Ochre, and White.

3

As can be seen in step three and in the finished painting, the background was kept quite deep in value to contrast with the white pitcher and jar. Both containers reflect the blue of the background drapery and the color of the lemons is reflected in the pitcher. In this analogous color scheme, the background color is more intense than both jar and pitcher but not so strong as to detract from the strong chromatic accents of the lemons and limes. The deep value in the jar also helps to accent the color of the fruit. Highlights were put in last in a manner that indicated the form of the object.

THALO GREEN
FRENCH ULTRAMARINE BLUE
YELLOW OCHRE WITH WHITE

YELLOW OCHRE
FRENCH ULTRAMARINE BLUE
WITH WHITE

YELLOW OCHRE
THALO GREEN
CADMIUM YELLOW, PALE

YELLOW OCHRE
CADMIUM YELLOW, PALE
FRENCH ULTRAMARINE BLUE

BURNT SIENNA
FRENCH ULTRAMARINE BLUE
WITH WHITE

BURNT SIENNA
FRENCH ULTRAMARINE BLUE
WITH WHITE

The physical act of mixing paint, applying it to the canvas, building surface texture, and blending and fusing colors can be an exciting experience that sometimes supersedes realism in the finished painting.

The freedom a painting knife offers for the application of color can be an interesting change from the brush; also, glazes can be applied to dry areas of paint with a piece of cotton rag and colors mixed and blended on the canvas with finger or thumb. Only the imagination of the painter limits the approach, restricts his technique, or dictates materials.

In the painting of roses on page 17, the flowers are part of an over-all composition of colors and textures rather than a specifically featured element of the painting.

In Step 1, the drawing was sketched on the canvas using Yellow Ochre thinned with turpentine. Then Step 2, color was blocked in on the over-all painting and, as the painting progressed, the possibilities for exciting textural effects in the background became more evident. As a result, the over-all surface texture gained in importance and in the finished painting the flowers were no longer as dominant as in the original conception.

The background is a subtle blending of colors used in the flowers and leaves kept low in intensity and value in order to accent the roses.

Note that in this and the preceding painting the most intense colors are restricted to a small portion of the painting. In the painting of the pitcher and jar it is the lemon and limes, and in this flower study, the color in the blossoms.

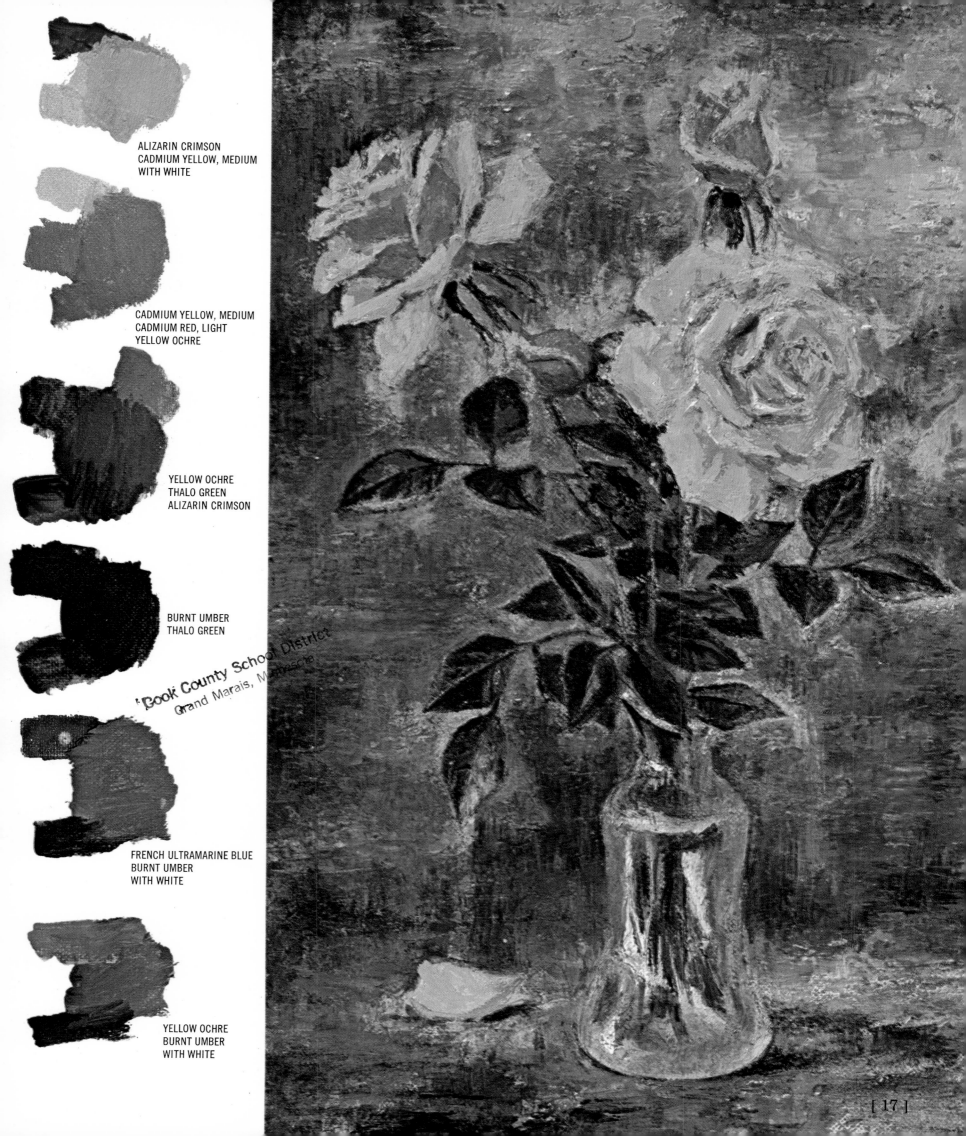

ALIZARIN CRIMSON
CADMIUM YELLOW, MEDIUM
WITH WHITE

CADMIUM YELLOW, MEDIUM
CADMIUM RED, LIGHT
YELLOW OCHRE

YELLOW OCHRE
THALO GREEN
ALIZARIN CRIMSON

BURNT UMBER
THALO GREEN

FRENCH ULTRAMARINE BLUE
BURNT UMBER
WITH WHITE

YELLOW OCHRE
BURNT UMBER
WITH WHITE

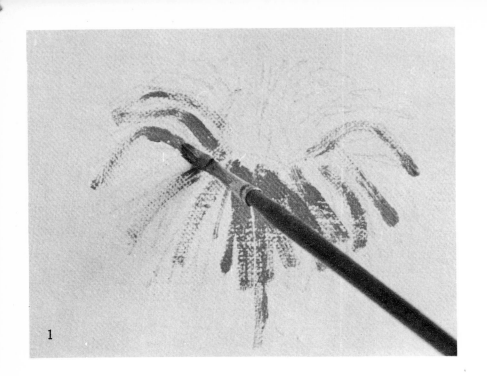

These illustrations show the painting development of two distinct types of blossoms: the Aster and the Lilac. These basic steps of blocking in the general shape, indicating shadow area for a feeling of form, and creating the higher values and accents can be used for painting any flower.

With the Aster, Step 1 was to block in the form by painting the petals from the center outward, employing a middle value of the color of the flower. In Step 2, darker values were painted in, still following the form, and in Step 3, lighter values start to give the blossom a feeling of volume. The final step was to blend colors where necessary and add accents of color to the completed painting for sparkle.

3

4

Step 1 in the Lilac, consists of painting the over-all shape of the blossom in a middle value of the color of the flower. The deeper values in Step 2 are put in next to indicate the shadow areas. In Step 3, the transition between the middle and dark values is blended with an intermediate color. As a final step, the higher values are painted following the shape of individual blossoms. These blossoms, although they are all quite light, should not be painted with the identical color. Some subtle variation in the higher values will avoid monotony and give the final painting a greater feeling of dimension.

3

4

Flower painting gives the artist the opportunity of using his colors in happy profusion. Cadmium Yellows, Oranges, and Reds give such flowers as Zinnias and Marigolds their hot, robust flavor while greens, blues, and Alizarin Crimson help handle the cooler tones of the Asters, Iris, and Lilacs. When painting flowers, pay attention to the over-all shape of the blossom and the definite pattern of its shadow. This is what gives each flower its distinctive shape and individual characteristics. In this painting, the light source is above and behind the subject and as a result almost all of the bouquet is in shadow. This makes an interesting study because the manner in which color is used must suggest the luminosity of the flowers and also indicate shadow areas. This subtle relationship

THALO GREEN
CADMIUM YELLOW, PALE
FRENCH ULTRAMARINE BLUE
WITH WHITE

is accomplished where the lighted areas blend into the shadow. It is here that the purest, brightest colors are used and these small touches suggest the over-all brightness of the subject. Likewise, the brass bowl gets its metallic characteristics by reflected light in the shadow area.

THALO GREEN
CADMIUM YELLOW, PALE
CADMIUM ORANGE

COBALT BLUE
YELLOW OCHRE
WITH WHITE

CADMIUM YELLOW, DEEP
ALIZARIN CRIMSON
WITH WHITE

THALO GREEN
ALIZARIN CRIMSON
CADMIUM YELLOW, MEDIUM

YELLOW OCHRE
FRENCH ULTRAMARINE BLUE
THALO GREEN
WITH WHITE

On the left is shown the preliminary lay-in of color. Within the essentially analogous color scheme of the finished painting, it has been possible to inject accents of pink and deeper red without disturbing the over-all effect. This works because the greatest area of the painting uses a basic color scheme and these accents are handled subtly.

The following demonstrations were prepared by John Albert Pucci, noted teacher and painter. Mr. Pucci, in his landscape painting, prefers to sketch and gather color notes on the spot and use them as a basis for painting in the studio.

In the preliminary step to the full color painting on pages 24-25 (shown below), the entire canvas was covered with a middle value mixture of Thalo Blue, Raw Umber, and Superba White. No attempt was made to put this down as a flat color, it was instead applied quite freely with the painting knife and spots where colors didn't mix too thoroughly were purposely allowed to remain. The overall texture and interest in this somewhat uneven underpainting made for intriguing effects when local color was applied over it.

In the detail above can be seen the freedom with which the brush and knife are used in applying color and the manner in which it is possible to take advantage of the exciting accidental effects of working over the rough ground color.

When the underpainting was dry, a round sable brush was used to sketch in the composition with a mixture of Thalo Blue and Raw Umber thinned with turpentine. After this, lighter areas were put in broadly with the painting knife. The underpainting color was allowed to come through where the knife hit only the high spots of the rough surface.

The distant trees and hills were put in with a bristle brush. Brushing color lightly with a bristle brush over this ground color can create diversified effects and indicate texture of trees, snow, and rocks. The dark shape of the barn was painted in the same color and value as the dark tree forms around and behind it. The warmer color accents in the barn and rocks were put in last.

SUPERBA WHITE WITH A
TOUCH OF THALO BLUE
AND RAW UMBER

THALO BLUE, WHITE AND A SPOT
OF FRENCH ULTRAMARINE BLUE

CADMIUM ORANGE AND
BURNT SIENNA

This basically analogous color scheme uses blues and greens predominantly with complementary accents of Cadmium Orange and Burnt Sienna.

WHITE WITH A TOUCH OF
THALO BLUE AND THALO GREEN

ALIZARIN CRIMSON,
THALO GREEN AND
CADMIUM RED, LIGHT

WHITE WITH A TOUCH OF
THALO GREEN AND RAW SIENNA

BURNT SIENNA, BURNT UMBER
AND CADMIUM RED, LIGHT

When doing quick sketches on the spot, I concentrate on the large foliage areas and pattern created by color and value changes. With my notes of the general range of values and colors, I can rearrange compositions for a more interpretive treatment of the subject in the studio.

A series of exploratory sketches, such as the two on the right, were done very freely with the painting knife using a variety of background colors to determine which was the best over-all middle value background to use for the final painting on page 29. In this manner, I was also able to decide exactly how I wanted to rearrange elements and what kind of over-all statement I wanted to make.

In the first sketch, shown above, I tried a pale ground color of Cadmium Red, Light but found it too intense for the additional play of high intensity color I wanted to use. In the second sketch I used Chromium Oxide Green with a little bit of Burnt Umber. Although the response in this case was more to my liking, I felt that the green detracted from the strong red-orange over-all color statement that I wanted to make. The degree of color intensity in this case was right but the hue was not.

For my final choice, I prepared a canvas in advance by covering it with a rough mixture of Burnt Sienna, Cadmium Red, Light and a slight amount of English Red (Light Red) to keep the first two colors from being too intense. This was allowed to dry thoroughly before the painting was started.

When I decided on the compositional arrangement that best suited me, I sketched it in with a round sable brush using Burnt Umber mixed with Permanent Green, Light and thinned with turpentine. (See Step 1 — page 28.) With a painting knife, I then proceeded to lay in the largest, most dominant over-all color statement of the foliage. For this, I used a mixture of Cadmium Orange and Burnt Sienna. Any of the drawing covered by this lay-in of color was roughly restated. This is only necessary to keep a guide for applying subsequent color areas. Actually, the final painting and manipulation of shapes and areas was done directly with the knife.

In Step 2, you will see the manner in which I continued to build up areas of color. By establishing a middle value to paint on, I was able to work up to lighter areas and back to the darker ones, manipulating these back and forth until I was satisfied with the general effect. Do not concentrate on any one area — work over the entire canvas to bring all sections along at the same time. In this way, you can balance color and make adjustments where necessary. When the general statement is satisfactory, finish up specific areas with the lightest and darkest accents put in last.

This painting uses an analogous color scheme with complementary accent of the most dominant color notes. (The most dominant note, orange, is accented by the blue — and the cool red of the barn acts as a complementary accent to the second most important color statement, the yellow green.) The painting was done almost exclusively with a painting knife.

This method of working relies on the manner in which paint is applied over the rough pre-painted background color for textural effects that suggest rather than completely define rocks, trees, etc. It is important that the composition be planned carefully and later statements made as freely and directly as possible.

Check the tinting strength of each color in small quantities to determine approximate amounts needed in each mixture. In this way, you will avoid mixing more than is needed for a given area.

ALIZARIN CRIMSON
RAW SIENNA AND
WHITE

PERMANENT GREEN, LIGHT
BURNT UMBER
RAW SIENNA AND
CADMIUM ORANGE
WITH WHITE

CADMIUM ORANGE
BURNT SIENNA
ENGLISH RED, LIGHT

CADMIUM YELLOW, LIGHT
CADMIUM ORANGE
ENGLISH RED, LIGHT

ALIZARIN CRIMSON
BURNT UMBER
CADMIUM RED, LIGHT

PERMANENT GREEN, LIGHT
CADMIUM YELLOW, LIGHT
RAW SIENNA

PERMANENT GREEN, LIGHT
RAW SIENNA
CADMIUM ORANGE
AND WHITE

For the painting shown in color on pages 32-33, I used the same approach as with the two previous demonstrations. With sketch pad and felt pen, I searched for interesting subjects along the Maine coast. My first sketch, at the top of the page, proved to be a successful composition so it was used for the final painting with the addition of some buildings and boats that I could relate. A later sketch of a lobster boat was used for the large boat element instead of the one in the original sketch. In addition to the sketches, I used the camera for reference on details, etc.

The finished painting was done on a pressed wood panel prepared with four coats of Hyplar Gesso. In preparing such a panel, the Gesso should be allowed to dry between coats and each succeeding coat brushed in a direction opposite the previous one.

When the Gesso was dry, I painted the panel with a mixture of Thalo Blue, French Ultramarine Blue, and Burnt Umber. This was brushed on with a size 16 flat bristle brush. When dry, I used a white pastel stick to sketch in the composition. In addition to linear aspects, I used the pastel to try a spotting of some of the masses, as can be seen in the step on the bottom of page 30.

I painted in all of the larger tonal areas of sky and water first. The buildings and foreground areas followed. The entire panel was developed as quickly as possible. Color and value should be balanced as the work goes along. No one section should be developed too far before getting a spotting of color over-all. I used a combination of painting knives and bristle brushes and in all of the areas let background color come through for richer textural effects. Where an area had too much texture, I reduced it later when the painting was farther along and I could check sections in relation to each other for color, value, and texture. The background color was left untouched for all of the darker masses in the painting.

The colors in the sky were a mixture of Thalo Blue, Burnt Umber, and white in varying degrees. In some spots, the blue is more predominant than in others. I wanted a dramatic effect so the sky was kept quite dark. In the water, I used Thalo Blue and white with touches of Permanent Green, Light and added more French Ultramarine Blue and Burnt Umber to this as I painted foreground areas. As you can see, no attempt was made to put down large flat areas of color. By applying color with the painting knife and varying the spots of color mixed with the Thalo Blue and white, I was able to get a great deal of variety and excitement in this section.

I wanted to maintain a salty, sunbleached, muted effect to the color in the boat, shack, and pilings, etc. so hues were neutralized slightly by mixing complements with white in varying degrees.

Dark accents, deeper than the color of the basic background mixture, were put in with Ivory Black.

I put the painting aside for a few days and then came back for a fresh look and made adjustments that seemed desirable.

The palette used was as follows:

Superba White	Cadmium Red, Light
Thalo Blue	Alizarin Crimson
French Ultramarine Blue	Raw Umber
Permanent Green, Light	Burnt Umber
Cadmium Orange	Ivory Black

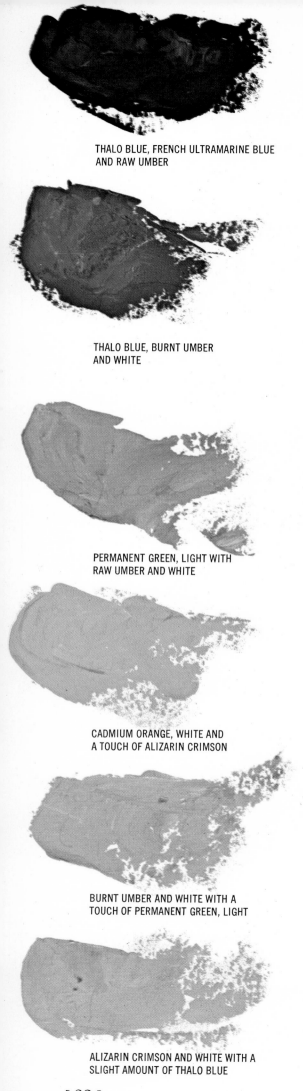

THALO BLUE, FRENCH ULTRAMARINE BLUE
AND RAW UMBER

THALO BLUE, BURNT UMBER
AND WHITE

PERMANENT GREEN, LIGHT WITH
RAW UMBER AND WHITE

CADMIUM ORANGE, WHITE AND
A TOUCH OF ALIZARIN CRIMSON

BURNT UMBER AND WHITE WITH A
TOUCH OF PERMANENT GREEN, LIGHT

ALIZARIN CRIMSON AND WHITE WITH A
SLIGHT AMOUNT OF THALO BLUE

ZINC YELLOW (LEMON YELLOW)
CADMIUM YELLOW, MEDIUM
CADMIUM RED, LIGHT
YELLOW OCHRE
BURNT SIENNA
BURNT UMBER
SUPERBA WHITE

ALIZARIN CRIMSON

THALO BLUE

FRENCH ULTRAMARINE BLUE

THALO GREEN

OIL CUPS

BASIC PALETTE

CADMIUM YELLOW, PALE
CADMIUM YELLOW, MEDIUM
CADMIUM RED, LIGHT
YELLOW OCHRE
RAW SIENNA
ENGLISH RED, LIGHT (LIGHT RED)
BURNT SIENNA
BURNT UMBER

ALIZARIN CRIMSON, GOLDEN

FRENCH ULTRAMARINE BLUE

SUPERBA WHITE

COBALT BLUE

THALO BLUE

OIL CUPS

PERMANENT GREEN, LIGHT

THALO GREEN

ADVANCED PALETTE

The importance of orderly working habits cannot be over emphasized. One that deserves great consideration is the arrangement of the colors on the palette. Developing a set pattern of putting the colors down permits concentration on the painting at all times without the distraction of having to stop and search for a certain color.

Colors can be arranged in a number of ways—a) warm on one side of the palette and cool on the other—b) in the order of the spectrum—c) in groupings according to intensity. The important thing is to decide on the one that best suits you. Keep your colors in that order each time you paint.

In the top photograph the basic palette described on page 3 is arranged with the warm colors running across the top edge and the cool colors down the side. In the bottom photograph is shown a more advanced palette and the position that additional colors would take utilizing the same warm-cool arrangement.

Some painters prefer to lay out a number of small dabs of each color rather than one large one. This is helpful in keeping colors clean.

Painting cups which clip to the palette, hold medium and turpentine. Half turpentine and half linseed oil makes a good mixture to use as a medium.

When you have finished working for the day, the mixing section of the palette should be scraped clean, white and any other color that is stained should be removed and the palette wiped with a rag. Since most oil colors remain usable for some time, any clean color can be left on the palette.

The impressive range of effects possible with oil color is determined to a large degree by the manner in which the paint is applied. The use of a painting knife for underpainting can leave a surface texture over which, when dry, color can be applied with a knife or brush which hits the high spots of the surface to effect changes in color. Scumbling, the application of additional color with a fairly dry brush, can give you softer textures and changes in color. Glazing with thin washes of color provides even more subtle color changes.

These photographs show some techniques which may be used:

The rag can be used for a soft blending of colors in certain areas. (See #1 above) Rags should be soft and absorbent—old shirts or worn sheets are quite good.

The painting knife is shown in #2 being used to scrape color from the painting to allow the texture of the canvas to show through for greater variety and interest in the area.

The bristle brush (#3) is shown being used to scumble fairly dry color over a previously painted section of the canvas which had dried.

In #4 a smaller painting knife is being used for the delicate application of color over an impasto section of the underpainting. The dark underpainting shows through for a variety of fascinating textures.

The following demonstration, through page 37, was prepared by Dean Ellis, a well-known painter whose work appears in many public and private collections.

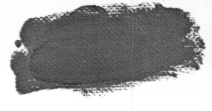

ALIZARIN CRIMSON AND BURNT UMBER WITH A SPOT OF IVORY BLACK

COBALT BLUE AND WHITE MODIFIED WITH IVORY BLACK

This abstract of surf and rocks was executed in oil on a pressed wood panel which had been prepared with Hyplar Gesso. As a preliminary to painting, the panel was covered with a ground color consisting of Burnt Umber, Thalo Crimson, and Mars Black. For this ground color, I used Hyplar polymer colors which make an excellent underpainting for oils and dry very rapidly. The color was brushed over the panel very loosely without regard to the ultimate design of the painting.

In Step 1, the basic masses were sketched in with a light pastel in the broadest possible terms. Next, the surface was sprayed with Retouch Varnish and the painting started. The purpose of the varnish was to 'fix' the pastel and to provide a slightly tacky surface into which I could work with oils. The sky, about a middle value equal to that of the background color, was laid in with a painting knife and rags, allowing the underpainting to show through in spots.

Next, in Step 2, the darker values were developed, and at the same time lighter color values introduced. The purpose was to move the painting as rapidly as possible to its

ultimate color and value range. The smaller, more detailed forms and subtle colors were developed in keeping with the desired feeling and mood. Painting knives were used to establish the linear pattern of the painting after the colors had reached a suitable degree of tackiness.

ULTRAMARINE RED, YELLOW OCHRE
AND A TOUCH OF BURNT UMBER

BURNT UMBER, THALO GREEN
AND YELLOW OCHRE

ULTRAMARINE RED, WHITE AND A
TOUCH OF ALIZARIN CRIMSON

ULTRAMARINE RED, COBALT BLUE AND
WHITE WITH A SPOT OF IVORY BLACK

Colors in the rock mass, derived from notes and recollections of rocks and algae along the shore, were held to darker values to imply solidity. As a final step, edges were given considerable attention, sharpening them in certain instances for maximum contrast and softening them in others for variety.

The oil color palette for this painting was as follows:

Superba White	Cobalt Blue
Cadmium Orange	French Ultramarine Blue
Yellow Ochre	Thalo Green
Alizarin Crimson	Ultramarine Red
Burnt Umber	Ivory Black

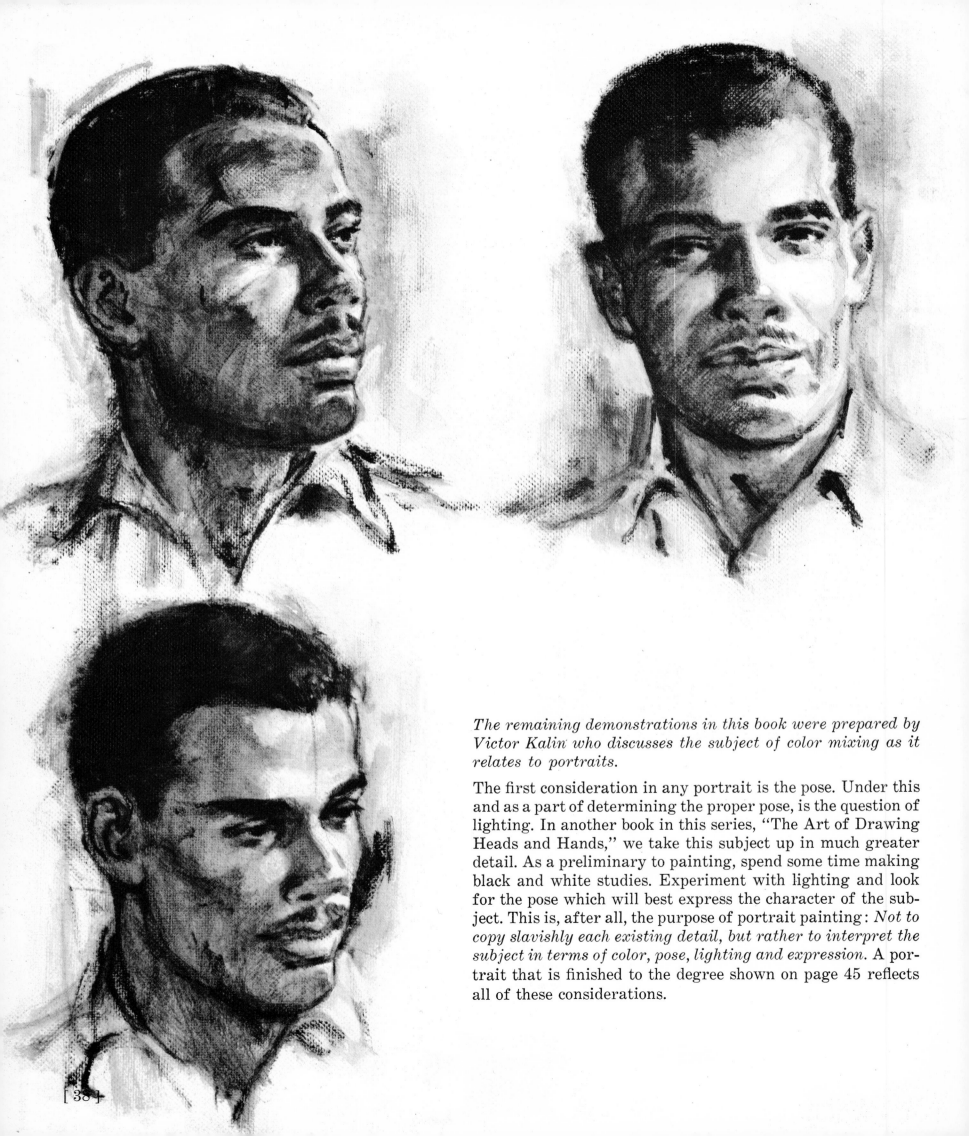

The remaining demonstrations in this book were prepared by Victor Kalin who discusses the subject of color mixing as it relates to portraits.

The first consideration in any portrait is the pose. Under this and as a part of determining the proper pose, is the question of lighting. In another book in this series, "The Art of Drawing Heads and Hands," we take this subject up in much greater detail. As a preliminary to painting, spend some time making black and white studies. Experiment with lighting and look for the pose which will best express the character of the subject. This is, after all, the purpose of portrait painting: *Not to copy slavishly each existing detail, but rather to interpret the subject in terms of color, pose, lighting and expression.* A portrait that is finished to the degree shown on page 45 reflects all of these considerations.

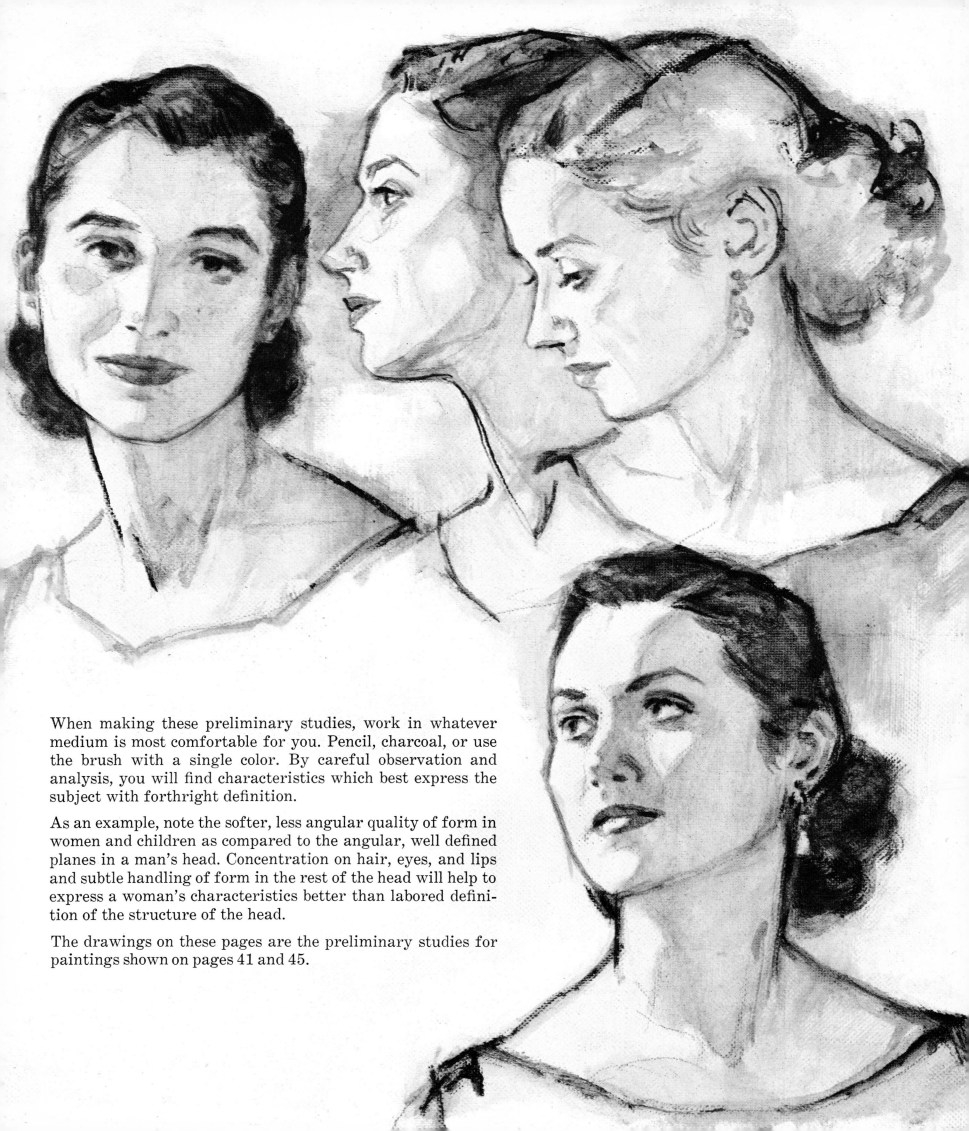

When making these preliminary studies, work in whatever medium is most comfortable for you. Pencil, charcoal, or use the brush with a single color. By careful observation and analysis, you will find characteristics which best express the subject with forthright definition.

As an example, note the softer, less angular quality of form in women and children as compared to the angular, well defined planes in a man's head. Concentration on hair, eyes, and lips and subtle handling of form in the rest of the head will help to express a woman's characteristics better than labored definition of the structure of the head.

The drawings on these pages are the preliminary studies for paintings shown on pages 41 and 45.

In this portrait, an analogous color scheme is used. The colors are within a very close range and values run a fairly complete range from dark to light.

1. The head was sketched in with a mixture of Raw Sienna and Burnt Sienna thinned with turpentine and the shadow areas put in with a heavier mixture of this same combination. The background was partially blocked in with a mixture of Yellow Ochre, Cadmium Yellow, Light, a touch of Thalo Green, and white. The shirt is a mixture of Alizarin Crimson and Cadmium Orange. The drawing was restated with a darker mixture of Burnt Sienna and Ultramarine Blue.

2. In this step, the complete blocking in of all the color areas prior to finishing up any one section can be seen.

The portrait was finished by refining areas, picking up accents, softening and blending edges where necessary and adding texture to the background by applying additional color with the painting knife.

BURNT SIENNA
YELLOW OCHRE
FRENCH ULTRAMARINE BLUE
WITH WHITE

YELLOW OCHRE
THALO GREEN
BURNT SIENNA

YELLOW OCHRE
CADMIUM YELLOW, PALE
THALO GREEN WITH WHITE

RAW SIENNA
BURNT SIENNA

FRENCH ULTRAMARINE BLUE
BURNT SIENNA

CADMIUM ORANGE
ALIZARIN CRIMSON

Children are probably the most difficult of models because their attention span is so short. They become bored with the business and tend to show this in their expressions. This is not necessarily bad and can quite frequently result in a more appealing portrait. Spend the time mixing colors while they are resting between poses.

A complementary color scheme was used for the portrait on page 44. The progressive steps in the development of the painting from a linear rendition to the massing of color are shown on the facing page.

The drawing in Step 1 was sketched in on the canvas with Yellow Ochre thinned with turpentine and as quickly as possible the white of the canvas was covered. For the background Thalo Green with a little Yellow Ochre was used and in the dark areas, some Burnt Sienna was added to this mixture. The shirt was a mixture of Cadmium Red, Light; Alizarin Crimson and Cadmium Yellow, Pale. The shadow areas of the face and hands were blocked in with Burnt Sienna; Cadmium Red, Light; Yellow Ochre and a touch of Thalo Green. After this the lighter flesh areas were put in using White mixed with very small quantities of Yellow Ochre; Cadmium Red, Light; Alizarin Crimson, and to cool this mixture slightly, a touch of Thalo Green.

In painting, you should carefully examine and indicate the shapes of the shadow areas. Generally, in portraiture, the shadows are painted cool to effect a contrast with the normally warm, lighter flesh tones. However, this relationship can be reversed. It is best to exclude white from dark shadow color mixtures. The amount of color needed in each mixture is best determined by mixing very small quantities in advance. For the lighter tints, start with white and add color slowly. For the darker, more chromatic colors, start with the most predominant color in the mixture and modify this carefully.

The painting was finished by blending areas between the light and dark, painting intermediate values in the light areas, and picking up accents wherever needed.

The palette used for this painting was: Superba White; Yellow Ochre; Cadmium Yellow, Pale; Cadmium Red, Light; Alizarin Crimson; Burnt Sienna; Burnt Umber; French Ultramarine Blue; and Thalo Green.

In the Portrait on page 45, the same palette was used. The model's opalescent skin tones are balanced by the stronger colors of her clothing. Basically, the shadows of the skin are cool, tending toward a soft violet gray. The addition of various reflected colors helps with the modeling and provides both interest and variety in the flesh areas.

Colors used on the background and clothing are shown next to the painting. The light flesh color was a mixture of white with very small quantities of Yellow Ochre; Cadmium Red, Light; Alizarin Crimson and to cool this slightly, Thalo Green was used. The soft violet grays in the shadow area are the result of mixing small quantities of Yellow Ochre; Alizarin Crimson; Burnt Sienna; and French Ultramarine Blue with white. Experiment with your mixtures for painting warm and cool shadow colors. The slight reduction in the intensity of a flesh color might be sufficient to indicate the turning of a plane.

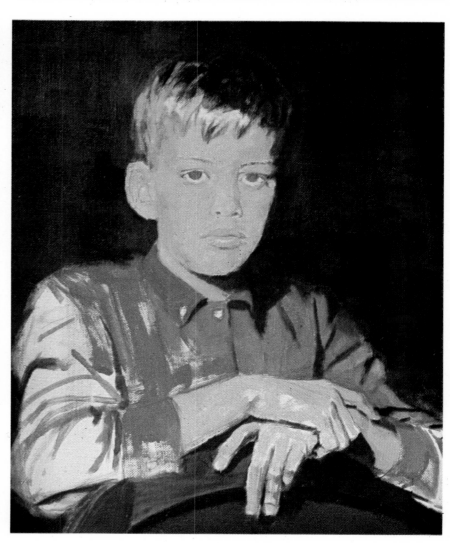

YELLOW OCHRE
BURNT SIENNA
THALO GREEN

THALO GREEN
YELLOW OCHRE
CADMIUM RED, LIGHT
ALIZARIN CRIMSON
WITH WHITE

BURNT SIENNA
ALIZARIN CRIMSON
THALO GREEN

ALIZARIN CRIMSON
BURNT UMBER

M. Grumbacher, Inc. manufactures a Flesh Color to simplify mixing when painting portraits. This color can be modified with additional color for a great variety of subtle skin tones. At the right, we show some of the many modifications possible.

FLESH

CHROMIUM OXIDE GREEN ADDED

FRENCH ULTRAMARINE BLUE
YELLOW OCHRE
THALO GREEN
WITH WHITE

CADMIUM RED, LIGHT
YELLOW OCHRE
THALO GREEN
ALIZARIN CRIMSON
WITH WHITE

YELLOW OCHRE
FRENCH ULTRAMARINE BLUE
ALIZARIN CRIMSON
BURNT SIENNA
WITH WHITE

CADMIUM YELLOW, PALE
CADMIUM RED, LIGHT
ALIZARIN CRIMSON
BURNT UMBER

YELLOW OCHRE ADDED

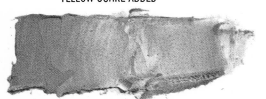

GRUMBACHER RED ADDED

MARS VIOLET ADDED

[45]

Photographs can be used to capture a pose when dealing with a restless subject. These should, however, be suplemented with your own careful observation and drawings. As can be seen in these pastel studies, the light and shadow areas have been kept as simple as possible, almost flat, and they still retain all the feeling of form necessary. Pastel is an ideal medium for quick color notes as well as more finished paintings.

An unusual method of handling a standard subject is by the use of back lighting. This throws the subject into shadow and the initial effect is a silhouetted shape against the background. This creates a challenging and interesting problem because the modeling of form must be accomplished by the most subtle changes in both color and value.

The basic flesh tones in the painting on page 48 are represented by the two upper mixtures. The uppermost, by introducing Alizarin Crimson, is cooler than the second employing Burnt Sienna. As flesh tones, they require little modification to achieve the range of values found in the face. The third mixture is basic for the darks. The fourth is for general light areas.

In an analysis of this painting, it can be seen that areas sparkle as the result of color similar in value and intensity but varying greatly in hue. The background is alive with tints of yellow, pink, green, blue, and brown, yet the over-all effect is of a single graded tone when seen from a distance. The same juxaposition of color is present throughout the painting. By maintaining a close value range within each area, it is possible to use a variety of color and still maintain a feeling of unity.

Start by blocking in general color areas as shown in the previous demonstrations and gradually build up texture with scumbling and glazing, adjusting areas to each other as you go along. Sections that seem too strong can be scraped or left to dry and then reworked to bring them back into balance.

The palette used for this painting was as follows:

Superba White	Burnt Sienna
Cadmium Yellow, Pale	Burnt Umber
Cadmium Red, Light	Thalo Green
Alizarin Crimson	Yellow Ochre
French Ultramarine Blue	

YELLOW OCHRE
CADMIUM RED, LIGHT
ALIZARIN CRIMSON
THALO GREEN
CADMIUM YELLOW, PALE

CADMIUM RED, LIGHT
YELLOW OCHRE
BURNT SIENNA
THALO GREEN
CADMIUM YELLOW, PALE

THALO GREEN
YELLOW OCHRE
ALIZARIN CRIMSON
BURNT UMBER

SUPERBA WHITE WITH
THALO GREEN
YELLOW OCHRE
FRENCH ULTRAMARINE BLUE
ALIZARIN CRIMSON

[48]